I0109098

THE REAL DEAL ABOUT MARRIAGE

MALINIA MCNEILL WOODS

©Copyright 2014, Malinia McNeill Woods, Miami, Florida. All rights reserved.

FOREWORD

After 30 years of marriage to one man, I have learned a thing or two about having success and happiness within the bounds of matrimony. These lessons have been learned through many trials, errors and victories that can be used to build a relationship that stands the test of time. The engagement of my oldest daughter inspired me to compile a list of lessons learned from marriage so that I could impart wisdom to my daughter and her fiancée. I wanted to provide them with information about marriage that I wished I had known at the beginning of my own married life. This book takes a humorous approach to marriage that will provide insight that can be used to help couples get to the pinnacle of happiness and become better people along the way. This information can be used by all married couples and engaged couples regardless of how long the relationship has been. The Real Deal About Marriage can also be used by marriage counselors, pastors, and other relationship professionals to provide modern day examples that can promote conversations necessary to heal relationships that are struggling or in need of a fresh perspective. The book can also be utilized in conjunction with biblical references to teach couples about the value of marriage and the importance of continued growth as a couple and as individuals. The Real Deal About Marriage presents an opportunity for dialogue between husbands and wives and can serve as a catalyst for changes in the marital relationship that can be beneficial to couples and families in general. Allow the information in this book to open your minds and encourage your hearts to see marriage as an adventure with great possibilities.

Contents

DEDICATION

This book is dedicated to my husband, Mr. Carl Woods Jr. Baby, after 30 years of marriage I still love waking up with you each day and I look forward to enjoying this journey of life. May the next 30 years be as awesome as the first.

Acknowledgement

I would like to express my gratitude to the many people who inspired me, acted as a sounding board for me and put up with my many requests while I was writing this book. To my family; thank you so much for listening and being an encouragement to me during a time in my life and marriage that I needed you. Thank you for pushing me forward and helping me to embrace the vision and the purpose for my life. I greatly appreciate all of you and love you more every day. I give all glory to God for His direction, revelation and blessings that only He can give.

A Little Background

As I said in the Foreword, my husband and I have been married for 30 years and we have been through some highs and lows. I was in the military for almost 22 years and my husband allowed me to pursue my career as an Army Warrant Officer while he worked as a Corrections Officer. This meant that each time my military career required me to relocate to a new duty station my husband would give up his current employment and seek employment at the new duty location. The experience of relocation tends to be the normal occurrence for military families; however, it was quite unusual for the wife to be the military member while the husband was a civilian. As a result of my military career in the United States Army, our family ended up relocating quite a bit. This took us to numerous overseas locations which included Berlin, Germany; Brunssum, The Netherlands;

Seoul, Korea; and several stateside locations including Fort Lee, Virginia; Fort Bragg, North Carolina; and Fort Rucker, Alabama. There were also many temporary duty assignments that required that I travel without my family. Some of the overseas temporary duty locations included Stockholm, Sweden; Brussels, Belgium; and Graffenwoehr, Germany. Each time the whole family relocated, my husband would give up his job and start over again in our new location. On some occasions he was able to find employment in similar career fields; however, on many occasions he would begin an entirely different job which made advancement difficult. Needless to say, relocating every few years made pursuing a consistent career very difficult for my husband. On at least one occasion he strongly considered remaining in the United States instead of moving to the next duty station.

Although remaining behind was an option, Carl always made the sacrifice and gave up his job to keep our family together.

Moving so often can take a toll on a family and definitely present challenges to a marriage. We went through some very turbulent times that caused us to question if we truly wanted to be married. There were times that we placed ourselves in compromising situations that caused marital discord. There were times that other people created drama that promoted chaos and challenged the trust in our relationship. There was even a time that I seriously contemplated divorce; to the extent that our marriage could have been dissolved in as little as 30 days!

Each of the experiences we had along the way taught us some lessons that we want to pass on to other married couples, engaged couples, or people who desire to eventually get married. The lessons we learned will be covered under six topics of discussion: communication, having some fun, sex, money, dreams and support of dreams, and finally, forgiveness.

Communication

The first step to having a successful and happy marriage is recognizing the importance of open communication. Ladies, men do not think the same way that we do and they are not mind readers! It is of critical importance that we let them know what we want, why we want it and how we expect to go about obtaining it. Open communication does not mean TALKING LOUD or interrupting the conversation to make your point. I must admit that I have a tendency to monopolize the conversation, especially when discussing something that I am passionate about. It's easy for me to take the vocal ball and run with it because my husband tends to be a bit quiet and more reserved. I recall when we first met more than 35 years ago; he had this quiet confidence about him that made me initially view him as being conceited. That quiet confidence was even more appealing to me because he also had beautiful eyes and broad shoulders; but I digress. I mentioned the differences between our approach to conversation and communication to stress how important it is to find your voice and make your wishes known. The key to having open communication is to listen, hear, process the information, develop an articulate response in your mind, and then speak in a calm manner. I know that sounds like a lot of trouble when it's so much easier to just speak your mind quickly or in a long-winded manner to make your intentions clear. But think about how many times you have spoken quickly and then regretted what you said. Once you say something, regardless of how badly you may feel about the words you used, you cannot get those words back. Ladies you should also know that long-winded speeches will not be effective either because the average man stops listening to you after the first minute anyway if the subject does not appeal to them. Men are more concerned about what you do than what you say. That is probably why there are so many instances in which men will keep trying to convince women to do something even after they initially say "no". It's not always what you say, but how you say it and more importantly, what you do after you say it.

If you have an issue that needs to be addressed, take some time to yourself to mull over your concerns before you present the issue to your spouse. That goes for both husbands and wives. It's a good idea to write down your concerns, come up with some options for dealing with the issues, and then analyze the options before making a joint decision. This approach will allow both parties to be involved in the decision making process and increases the possibility of coming to a decision that won't cause problems for either spouse. Writing things down then coming back to review them much later will give you the opportunity to reflect on what you are really trying to say and help to ensure that you do not speak out of anger or hast. It will also give you a chance to make sure that your suggestions are relevant and realistic. I recall a time that my husband and I were going through a bit of a rough patch. I had returned from a six month overseas tour and my husband had made some decisions that I did not agree with. I became very emotional and totally over reacted to the situation. My husband observed my behavior and made it his priority to diagnose what my problem was and come up with a solution. His intention was good but the manner that he elected to communicate his thoughts to me left a lot to be desired and actually caused more problems than solutions. After doing some research on women's health issues, my husband thought that he had determined the cause of my emotional response and proceeded to explain to me that I was suffering from a chemical imbalance and all I needed was medication. As you can probably guess, this did not go over very well at all. I don't recall my exact words but suffice it to say, they were not flattering at all and was borderline profanity. I'm sure my husband wished that he had written down the information he wanted to present to me and reviewed it carefully to make sure that his message didn't insinuate that he thought I was crazy, even though he probably thought I was. A better way to approach the situation would probably be to just give me a warm embrace and tell me he was sorry that I was upset. Now doesn't that sound better than saying he thinks I need to be medicated?

Guys, make sure you contribute to the conversation by providing "constructive" input. It is not acceptable to always respond with " I don't care; whatever you want to do". Contrary to popular belief, the average wife wants her husband to have an opinion and a backbone. Simply responding with, "yes dear" every time your wife speaks may make it easier to keep an argument from occurring but that response is not an effective long term solution to anything. Find that happy medium between being a doormat and being a bully. You will know when you have found the right mix because your wife will respond in a manner that shows her appreciation or disdain depending on your success or failure. The same applies in reverse order. That old saying "when momma is not happy, no one is happy ", is generally a very true assessment. Take the time to really communicate and let your spouse know that you value their opinion but you also have your own opinion. Sometimes there will be a difference of opinion and that is okay. Just make sure that both parties make a genuine effort to be open and honest. I must say that my husband definitely voices his opinion and I have learned to slow my response and digest all the information that he shares before we make the joint decision to do things my way. That was an attempt at humor by the way.

Have Some Fun

Now that you have figured out how to communicate with your spouse without starting a war, the next step to having a successful and happy marriage is to have some fun. Don't worry guys; fun doesn't always translate into spending a lot of money. If you live close to the beach, get up early one weekend; pack a lunch, a blanket and head to the ocean. Spend some quality time together. Don't talk about work or any problems. You don't even need to talk at all! Just enjoy the sun, the water, and each other. If you don't live near the beach, go to a park, a sporting event, or simply go to your back yard. It doesn't really matter where you go or what you do as long as you do it together. If your budget will allow for something bigger or more involved; plan a trip or outing with your spouse. Make sure the event is something that both of you enjoy. Whatever you decide to do and wherever you decide to go, make it fun and memorable. Take pictures, make scrapbooks , or collect souvenirs to mark the occasion. There is something special about looking back at mementos that have been collected over time.

Husbands and wives need to remember the types of activities they engaged in when they initially began dating each other. I'm not suggesting that you can go back in time; however, I am suggesting that you can begin again. If dancing was your thing back in the day, then sign up for a salsa class or whatever style of dance intrigues you both. If going to movies was the activity of choice when you were dating, then head to the theatre. Make date night a regular part of your weekly activities. Re-kindle that spark that was so exciting when you were dating and don't let the fire burn out. Take turns planning the activity for date night and keep it interesting. Now ladies, I know that many of us like to be in charge of planning the activities because we like to have things a certain way and we like to make sure that everything is organized. Please resist the temptation to always be the one who has to be in charge of the activities for date night. Both the husband and wife should have ideas for things they would like to do or places to go. Now ladies, please give your husbands a little room for improvement on his choices for date night and don't be too quick to judge. Some guys have a tendency to look at date night activities solely from their perspective and may need a little time to get the point of the endeavor. Guys, take the time to research potential date night activities and make the effort to keep things interesting to both you and your wife. You will be greatly rewarded if you show your spouse that you value the time that you spend with them and you are sensitive to their desires. You are only limited by your imagination and your budget. Speaking of budget, don't allow what you observe on social media or on reality TV to influence you to live beyond your means. You can have fun without breaking the bank and you definitely don't need to take any lessons from reality television in that regard. Keep in mind that reality TV has major sponsorship and none of the characters are paying for anything out of their own pockets. Google things to do in your area and take advantage of cultural events that expose you to new and interesting things. As I said, you can have fun without breaking the bank; however, you should also set an appropriate budget and avoid complaining about the cost. Guys, your wives want to feel special and appreciated. A sure way to defeat the purpose of date night is to openly complain about the cost or make physical gestures that reveal your dissatisfaction with the bill for the activities. Don't openly gasp or choke on your beverage when you get the bill. Doing so would draw unnecessary attention and could be quite embarrassing. The whole point of date night is to spend quality time with each other. Complaining about how much money you are spending is a sure way to diminish that quality. In fact, complaining about the money you are spending can send the message that you place little value on your spouse and don't think she is worth the cost.

All married couples go through periods of time in the marriage when there doesn't seem to be enough time in the day to really spend time together. Some of us have professions that take up quite a bit of our time and some of us have responsibilities that are very demanding. If this is the case for you please pay special attention to this section. Ask yourself what your priority is and what your priority should be. Your spouse and your family should be among your top priorities and your job should not take their place. I realize that there are jobs that are very important due to the nature of the occupation and its impact on society overall. Doctors, lawyers, pastors, military members and public safety personnel; are all professions that can take up a great deal of time, energy, and effort. I don't mean to downplay the importance of these positions; however, I do believe that your marriage is just as important and warrants that time be spent in developing it to reach its full potential. All of the professions mentioned here require periodic recertification, training, and license that are mandatory in order to continue to serve in those capacities. If a doctor does not stay informed about new medical procedures or treatment he or she could jeopardize the life and well-being of their patients. If a lawyer doesn't keep up to date on cases that have changed the way that laws have been interpreted, he or she can jeopardize the freedom of their client. Likewise if husbands and wives do not stay informed and up to date about the things concerning their marriage and family, they are placing their marriage in jeopardy and are at risk of causing it to fail. Regardless of your occupation you have to make time for your spouse and you must do so on a consistent basis. It is crucial to the welfare and survival of your marriage that you stay involved and interested in what your spouse needs from you. Don't put the needs of others before those of your spouse and don't become so disconnected that you do not notice that your spouse is not happy with the relationship. Get back to the basics and put the fun back in your marriage. Now pastors, I know you have a duty to look out for the spiritual wholeness of your church members and you have an obligation to provide sound counsel, and spiritual development to the flock you are responsible for; however, you are not exempt from the responsibility that you have to your husband or wife. There is an old saying that is appropriate for this situation. "Don't be so heavenly minded that you are no earthly good." Take your role as a pastor very seriously, but do not neglect your marriage in the process. Don't forget that you are human and are prone to human weaknesses that could potentially cause issues in your marital relationship. You should be cautious about how counseling is conducted with your church members, especially with members of the opposite sex. I know that counseling sessions require privacy and confidentiality; however, counseling also requires using wisdom. Wisdom is the beginning of understanding and it is so important for pastors to use wisdom to understand the needs of their members as well as their motives. We would like to think that anyone seeking spiritual counseling has only good intentions but that would be naive. Psalms 118:8 says, "It is better to take refuge in the Lord than to trust in man." Pastors, be sure to establish some policies and procedures for providing counseling services at your church. I would suggest having your spouse present during counseling sessions. This would be beneficial to both the pastor and the church member because it would ensure that everything is conducted in an orderly fashion that leaves no room for suspicion or misunderstandings.

Now I'm sure some of you couples are asking yourself a few questions by now. Am I supposed to spend all my free time with my spouse? Can't I have friends and do things with my friends that don't include my spouse? What about spending time by myself? My answer to these questions are no, yes, and sure you can. No; you are not supposed to spend all your free time with your spouse. Marriage doesn't chain you to your spouse on a day in day out basis. It is perfectly okay to take part in activities that do not include your spouse; however, these activities must be of the sort that does not dishonor your spouse or the bonds of your relationship. If you want to join a sports league, a book club, or train for a marathon that's absolutely fine. The problem comes in when spouses have ulterior motives that could cause marital problems. You know the types of extracurricular activities that a married person should not engage in; so I will not insult your intelligence. You can definitely have friends and do things with your friends that don't include your spouse; however, those activities must not dishonor your spouse or jeopardize the trust of your relationship. Don't place yourself in a position for suspicion. There is a biblical scripture that says "don't give the devil a foothold". In other words, don't give evil an opportunity. You've heard the phrase that someone is "asking for trouble" when they do and say things that will bring the wrong kind of attention their way. If you are married and committed to having a happy marriage, you will refrain from activities and friends that are incidents just waiting to happen. Spending time alone is just fine as long as the time you spend alone is not spent in a self-destructive manner or in an unhealthy manner. Everyone should spend some time alone reflecting on life, establishing personal goals and contemplating your future. Every waking moment does not have to be spent with your spouse and if you feel the need to always cling to your husband or wife, you may have some issues that need attention. It's one thing to be in love with your spouse and enjoy spending time with them. It's a totally different thing to obsess over your spouse and need to call them every minute they are away from you. If the latter applies to you, please get some professional help before your obsession evolves into an unhealthy situation warranting intervention.

Sex, Sex and More Sex

Now we come to the subject that is crucial to the success and happiness of a marriage; sex. Yes, sex! This subject is something that many people avoid discussing with their spouse. This is one of those areas that many women assume should be the sole responsibility of the husband. Ladies, remember what I said about a man thinking differently and not being able to read our minds? The subject of sex is a prime example of when we should let our husband know what we want, why we want it and how we expect to go about obtaining it. I don't mean to bark orders at your spouse or be overly aggressive; unless that's what you both are into. What I mean is to be intimate with your spouse. Let him know what you like and how certain things make you feel. Guys, sex is all about intimacy for the average women. We like to know that you enjoy what we do, how we do it, and we also want to know what you really want in the bedroom or whatever room. If there is something that you want, let your spouse know. If there is something that you don't want, let that be known too.

Ladies, sex for the average husband is more about quantity than quality and that is ok. You can increase the quantity without diminishing the quality. It's not always about being able to "go all night" especially as we get further along in age. Quickies can be extremely intense and satisfying if we include some special effects. Special effects are only limited by our imaginations and our openness to exploration. Now I don't mean to imply that you should delve into the underworld of kinkiness, unless that's what you both are into. However, there are a few "KY" commercials that come to mind that are quite popular and effective. Be unselfish with your spouse and be attentive to what their needs are. If both the husband and wife commit to making sure that the other party is satisfied in the bedroom, there will be fewer disagreements in any other room.

Sex is so important to a marriage that any issue in that department needs to be addressed promptly. If either the husband or wife has experienced some changes in libido, a doctor should be consulted. This is another area where open communication will come in handy. There is nothing taboo or inappropriate about discussing changes in sex drive. There is also nothing wrong with filling a prescription if necessary to ensure that both the husband and wife are able to adequately participate in the festivities. Husbands should not avoid talking to their physician about any problems that they may be experiencing that could be a hindrance to sexual participation and performance. Please don't take that "rub some dirt on it" mentality that contributes to avoidance. In fact, consulting a medical professional about sexual dysfunction could reveal medical issues that could even be lifesaving.

Don't take any chances with your health. The same applies to women; however, women are more likely to seek medical intervention sooner than the typical man. Thankfully, my husband and I are both healthy and blessed to have no problems with our libido even after all these years together. This reminds me of a conversation I overheard between two elderly women in a beauty salon many years ago. They were discussing marriage and one lady stated that she and her husband slept in a king sized bed and they each stayed on their respective sides of the bed. The other lady responded by saying, "Don't you roll over there every now and then?" When the first lady said that she did not, the second lady said, "I'm 75 years old and I still have to roll over there every now and then." My husband and I are very thankful that our entire king sized bed gets utilized on a regular basis and we hope to have the same appetite in our golden years.

Sex is something that many married women don't like to discuss with their spouses because it makes them feel self-conscious. Most women will openly discuss sex with their girlfriends so why is it a problem to talk about it with their husbands? One of the appeals of talking about sex with our girlfriends is that it gives us a sounding board. When we talk with other ladies it gives us a chance to see that other people are dealing with some of the same issues as we are. We feel more inclined to share our feelings with our girlfriends because they can give us feedback from the perspective of another woman. Ladies, don't shy away from having those same conversations with your spouse. You may be pleasantly surprised to know that he may have some of the same concerns or desires.

Now this point that I am about to make may step on some toes; so if it does, just say ouch and keep on reading. Husbands and wives please don't become so comfortable with yourselves that you begin to get lazy with your appearance. I know that it can be difficult to balance everything on your plate. Many husbands and wives work outside of the home and inside of the home. Husbands and wives have responsibilities that make it difficult to make time for each other, but you have to do it. You have to place a priority on taking care of the total package; mind, body and spirit.

Ladies, take a good look in the mirror. If you see things about yourself that you are unhappy about, spend some time and effort on changing it. Husbands, if you don't quite have the abs you desire, work on it. We all have either gained weight in places we don't want to; lost weight in places we don't want to; lost hair in places we don't want to; grown hair in places we don't want to; or changed in some way over the years and that is absolutely natural. However, we all must make the effort to always put our best foot forward and we should have enough respect for ourselves and our spouses to always present our best selves. Guys, if your hairline has receded so much that it begins parallel to your ears, just go ahead and shave it off. Bald is sexy but only if you commit to it. Ladies, if gravity has begun to take its toll, make an investment into a good support system; Spanx. Our body is a temple and we should take every measure to keep the maintenance up to date. Now I'm not suggesting that we run to the plastic surgeons to lift this or tuck that or inject whatever. Cosmetic surgery is a choice that personally doesn't appeal to me; however, there is nothing wrong with taking care of our bodies and there is nothing wrong with dressing up our temple.

Most couples have a tendency to get a bit lazy with their appearance after being married for a while but that is the wrong thing to do. My father-in-law gave me a sound piece of advice when my husband and I got engaged. He said, "the same things it takes to get them, it takes to keep them". So ladies, if you used to take time and effort with your appearance prior to marriage you need to continue those same efforts after marriage. If you use to cook, clean or do other such things prior to marriage, you must continue to do so after marriage. If there were certain things that you use to engage in sexually with your man prior to marriage, guess what; those same things are expected after marriage. Guys, the same applies to you. If you use to conduct certain grooming habits, wear nice smelling colognes or engage in specific sexual activities with your lady prior to marriage, you have to keep those same fires burning. Now there are probably some married couples that did not engage in sexual activity with each other before marriage; so for the hand full of you that this topic doesn't apply to, feel free to skip forward to the next section. For those of you who are still reading this section, I offer this analogy. Think of it this way; if you were considering buying a house and it had beautiful marble floors, crown moldings, and a grand staircase to the second floor, you would expect those same features to be present once you bought the house. You would be ready to file a lawsuit if you bought the house but once you began to move in all the marble floors and crowning moldings had been removed and there was no access to the second floor because the grand staircase had been replaced with a step ladder. So husbands and wives, please make sure that you conduct routine maintenance on yourselves so that you don't end up getting sued for false advertising or violating the lemon law. I'm not by any means suggesting that we should trade in our spouses like used cars because things change in our personal appearance. Quite the contrary; I am suggesting that we treasure our spouses and ourselves so much that we make every effort to keep ourselves in pristine condition with all the original components.

Money

Money is the next subject that is important to marital success and happiness. This doesn't mean that you have to be "Oprah rich" to be happy in a marriage. Money is an important part of marriage because it is a subject that can lead to disagreements, arguments, and discord. How much money you have is not what is so important; however, how you manage the money you have is extremely important. Talk to your spouse about your financial goals and come to an agreement as to how you both can successfully attain those goals.

Ladies, I feel your pain. We all would love to have an unlimited supply of Coach purses, Christian Louboutin shoes, and diamonds from Tiffany's, but let's accept the fact that we are not rolling like that; yet. Be realistic in your approach and don't get so heavily invested in chasing the almighty dollar that you neglect the other important areas of your marriage. You can't have caviar dreams if you have a French fries budget and you shouldn't try to live like the Jones' when your name is Smith. Recognize what you are working with and make it work for you.

Money is an important factor in a marriage and can be a major sticking point. Many husbands and wives have varied ideas about who is in charge of the money and what is considered "my money, your money, and our money". Many couples have the opinion that all money should be joined together and that it should not matter who contributes what. I agree that it shouldn't matter how much money each spouse contributes to the household budget; however, I think that it is essential that whatever is contributed represents a significant amount of the total income from all sources. In my opinion there is no such thing as "my money or your money". In my opinion all the income between a husband and wife is just that; between a husband and wife. It doesn't matter who is responsible for creating the debt or who is to blame for increasing the amount of money owed. I know some of you may be thinking that the person who made the debt should be solely responsible for it and in theory you would be correct. However, in a marriage, debt will impact both the husband and the wife. Look at it like this; if the kitchen sink is full of dirty dishes it makes no sense to just pick out the cup you used and wash it. Sure, your cup may be clean; but the rest of the dishes will eventually begin to stink. Look at your debt just like that sink of dirty dishes and clean it up. Both the husband and wife should commit to becoming financially stable; otherwise your credit will start to stink just like those dirty dishes.

It's a fact that debt can negatively affect your marriage because it can become a bone of contention. It is so important to consult each other and make joint decisions about the financial goals you desire to achieve. Couples should never enter into major financial commitments without consulting each other and considering the impact the debt will have on your overall financial freedom. Luke 14:28 (NLT) says, "But don't begin until you count the cost. For who would begin construction of a building without first calculating the cost to see if there is enough money to finish it? " Take time out to talk about money concerns and don't give in to impulsive purchases that defeat your financial plans.

Neither of the spouses should spend money in a reckless manner and neither spouse should be overly selfish with money. Ladies, I know that it's important to pamper yourself; however, you should taper your spending to a manageable level that is appropriate for the overall budget. You should not be spending money on hairdos, manicures and pedicures if your electricity is in danger of being turned off at home. What good does it serve for you to look like a celebrity if you're sitting in the dark when you get home? You should not be buying clothes and shoes if your refrigerator and cabinets are bare. It's hard to look cute when your stomach is growling. Guys, you should not be spending money on video games, sporting equipment or other vices if your car insurance is about to lapse. "Grand Theft Auto" will not pay your insurance claim if you get into an accident. You should not be buying lottery tickets if you have to use the small change from the car ashtray or cup holder to do so. Wrap those quarters and put them in the bank to draw guaranteed interest rather than hoping to pick the right six numbers in the lottery.

Spending money recklessly or overly selfishly will lead to problems eventually. Always think about your financial goals and utilize money in a way that contributes to the financial plan. It's easy to get off track with how we spend money if we do not make a conscious effort to stick to a budget. You can easily be surprised by how much money is spent frivolously if you don't lay out a spending plan. My guilty pleasure happens to be high heeled shoes. For a long period of time I made a habit of going to my favorite shoe store at least twice each week and each time I would purchase shoes; sometimes two or three pair at once. I became such a regular that the sales staff knew me by name and was always quick to bring me the latest arrivals in my size without me having to ask. At the time I had not penned a budget plan and I was spending far more than I was aware of. Once I became aware of my spending, I decided to limit my shoe buying. I did not go to my favorite shoe store for at least six months. When I finally went back to the store, there was a big sign that said, "Going Out of Business". When one of the sales ladies saw me, she ran up to me and asked me where I had been. Now I don't claim to be the sole reason that the store closed their doors, but I'm certain that the money I use to spend there was greatly missed.

The shoe store incident caused me to really reflect on money management and not only budget for every expense, but stick to the budget that was set. If one spouse is better at managing money than the other then let that spouse take the helm. It is not a sign of weakness to allow your husband or wife to manage the checkbook if they have the knack for it. My husband was so great at managing money that we were able to wipe out our debt and buy our first house very early in our marriage. Money management is something that has to be consistently monitored and documented. It is not a good idea to spend money without immediately balancing the checkbook and noting the expense. Don't rely solely on your online banking options to keep a record of your spending. Some transactions can take quite a bit of time to post to your account and if you do not keep a real-time record of your spending you will end up forgetting to do so and possibly have a negative experience and a negative balance. It can be quite embarrassing for your credit card or debit card to be declined at the checkout register of a department store or in a restaurant because you didn't manage your account properly.

Set spending allowances for the things that are needed and set separate spending allowances for the things that are wanted. There is a major difference between a need and a want. Ladies, many of us want new clothes, shoes, purses and jewelry on a regular basis. Guys, many of you want a new car, motorcycle, stereo equipment or a big screened TV. While it is okay to want things, it is not okay to get things we want at the expense of not getting the things we need. We need a place to live so what sense would it make to spend rent money on a new pair of Manolo's. We need food to sustain our lives so what sense would it make to spend grocery money on a new set of car stereo speakers. I know some of you are telling yourselves that you work hard so you are entitled to have nice things for yourself. I concur; however, you must decide what your ultimate goal is and make the required sacrifices to reach your ultimate goal. My husband and I wanted to build a new home before I retired from the military. We decided that we would postpone purchasing new vehicles so that we could build the home we wanted. That meant that we continued to drive the same cars for another five years because we did not want to have car payments. People would ask us why we didn't buy a Mercedes or a BMW. My response, "Our Fords are still getting us from A to B without any problems and we can park them in the garage of our new house." So don't worry about appearances or temporary delays in reaching your financial goals. I would rather have money in the bank than to live from pay check to pay check trying to measure up to other people's standards.

Make a financial plan and consider the plan before making any impulse purchases. My mother always said not to go grocery shopping when you are hungry because you will spend more money on things that you don't really need. I suggest that if a person doesn't have non-committed money to spend then don't even go window shopping. That way you avoid having the devil versus angel debate. You know that ethical debate you have with yourself where the devil on your shoulder says, "go ahead" and the angel says, "don't do it". Avoid the temptation by staying out of the stores when you are not shopping purposely.

Dreams and Support of Dreams

The next area to cover in order to have a successful and happy marriage is two-fold; dreams and support of dreams. We all have had dreams about what we wanted to be, where we wanted to go and what we wanted to do. A successful and happy marriage includes having the ability and willingness to dream and support the dream. This is another area where a dose of reality is necessary. If you can't carry a tune in a bucket, you should not dream of becoming the next Mariah Carey or Brian McKnight. If you have a talent, gift or idea that you are passionate about, go for it. If your spouse has any of these type dreams or aspirations, support their efforts. Be patient with your spouse in the pursuit of their dreams and they will return the favor. On that same note, don't be a dream-killer. Encourage your spouse to pursue their dreams and give them your unconditional support. Those of us who have children would probably have no issue with encouraging them to work hard and telling them they can achieve anything they want; however, we don't always extend that same support and encouragement to our spouses. Make a conscious effort to fan the flames of passion as it relates to the dreams of our spouses and keep the fire burning. Eventually, dreams will materialize and if they don't; the marriage will still be warm and toasty. If your spouse supports your dream, let them know that their efforts are appreciated. Don't take the support for granted. Make the commitment to do everything reasonably possible to make the dream a reality. This shows your spouse that you are sincere in your efforts and it will help your spouse to remain supportive of your venture. I am so thankful that my husband has always supported my dreams and aspirations and given me every opportunity to make my dreams a reality. As I mentioned previously, my husband supported my military career and allowed me to reach every goal that I set at the expense of putting his own dreams on hold. I am now able to return the favor by supporting his musical endeavors and I have been rewarded by seeing and hearing the wonderful compositions that he has created. I am so proud of him for taking the time and putting in so much hard work to make his dream a reality.

If your dream is to get a college degree or pursue a particular career then you should get started on it right away without further delay. Continuing education is a good way to improve your ability to reach your financial goals. It is important to support your spouse in their educational endeavors but it is also important to have a realistic expectation of the outcome. Education can increase the possibility of landing that dream job but you have to proactively pursue that job; not wait for the job to come to you. Likewise, it is important that you have a goal in mind and commit to reaching the goal.

Don't spend your time and your money on obtaining a degree if you have no intention of utilizing the degree to obtain employment or start a business that will eventually improve your financial position. It is unfair to expect a spouse to financially support your dream if the reality doesn't make your life better. Why would you spend eight years in medical school if you didn't want to become a doctor once you completed? Why would you spend money and time obtaining a business degree if you had no intention of starting a business or working in business? There has to be a financial incentive or a personal benefit that would justify the support of a dream. Otherwise it would be a selfish action to utilize family funds in a way that does not benefit the family.

Forgiveness

Forgiveness is the final ingredient required for a successful and happy marriage. Even if we follow every step previously mentioned, there still will be issues that arise that have the potential to derail your happy marriage. In most instances these issues will involve one or more of the subjects we already talked about; communication, fun, sex, money, or dreams. In the event that there is a problem, address it head on. Talk about it and if necessary, get professional help with dealing with the issue.

Infidelity ranks highly as the culprit that leads to the destruction of a marriage and it is a subject that creates so many other problems that can contribute to the demise of marital bliss. Infidelity is not something that most couples intentionally set out to do; however, it is something that many couples continue to do if not properly addressed initially. When a couple gets married they normally intend to be monogamous, unless they both agree to something different. I'm not judging, but it seems like a waste of time, money and energy to get married if you fully intend to sleep around. Again, I'm not judging, so if that's what you are into, there should be no issue in the infidelity department unless there are some rules involved that may have been violated. I'm not familiar with the etiquette that dictates to swingers; so I can't speak on that issue. Whatever the case, forgiveness is the key to recovering from the betrayal of infidelity. Now you may be thinking that infidelity is the unforgivable sin that is guaranteed to end a marriage regardless of how much time has been invested; however, I can speak from personal experience that it does not have to be the case.

My husband and I went through a series of events that had the potential to not only end our marriage but end our lives as we knew it. Infidelity reared its ugly head during a time in our marriage that we were busy being preoccupied with other things in life. It's easy to say how you would react in a situation of this nature but you never really know until you are faced with it. Suffice it to say that going through issues of infidelity first hand gives you a whole new appreciation of the thin line between love and hate; or I should say the thin line between sanity and insanity. Violence has never been a part of my normal character but I can tell you that I'm thankful that I did not have a weapon readily accessible during this critical time of decision-making. Otherwise, I would have been writing this book from behind bars and my outlook on marriage would probably be very different. I look back at the situation now and I am able to laugh about it; but it was far from funny at the time. I shared all that just to let you all know that things are not always as bad as you initially perceive them to be and if you take the time to think things through without the emotion attached to it, you can come to a rational decision. This only works if both the husband and wife are willing to openly discuss the issues and determine the next course of action. I had to take a good look in my own closet and see the skeletons that I had hidden there. I had to realize that although my skeletons may not have been revealed, they still played a vital role in the situation that unfolded. There is a biblical principle that relates to sowing and reaping and it is very appropriate here; we reap what we sow. When we sow seeds in the soil and they receive the proper nourishment, they eventually grow into the type of produce they originally were. Once we sow the seeds we can no longer control them. We can't force the seeds to become something different once they have been planted. The same applies to our actions. Once we partake in certain activities we can't change them and we can't control the repercussions from them; however we can make different decisions in the future.

Husbands, if you have been unfaithful and genuinely want to save your marriage, listen closely. You have to be willing to talk to your wife and answer every question she has openly, honestly, and as many times as she asks. Don't sugar-coat the truth regardless of how hurtful and painful the truth may be. Don't insult your wife's intelligence by trying to tell her what you think puts you in the best light. Take full responsibility for the part you played in the betrayal and do not try to blame others for decisions you made. Guys, there are a few responses that your wife does not want to hear and you will make matters worse for yourself if you say any of these statements. "I don't know what I was thinking; it didn't mean anything to me; I couldn't control myself; it's not my fault; a man has needs." Making any of these statements has the potential to lead to a shouting match. However, you are placing yourself in danger of serious bodily injury if you shrug your shoulders in response to her questions! Shrugging your shoulders is the equivalent of saying you don't really care about having this conversation and you consider the whole issue as a waste of your time. If that is the message you are trying to convey; go ahead, shrug your shoulders. Hopefully, you will be ready to discuss the situation more openly once you awaken from being knocked out.

Husbands, you do not have the luxury of deciding when you have talked about the subject enough if you were the one who was unfaithful. You also are not in a position to determine what penalties will be assessed or choose which penalties you will accept. If your wife decides that she wants you to wine her, dine her and pamper her until she feels vindicated or wants you to do something else to prove to her that you will not become a repeat offender; then you will just need to suck it up and deal with it. Don't be so arrogant to think that you are such an awesome catch that your spouse should just be glad to be with you. Don't think so highly of yourself that you actually think that all you need to do is apologize and your wife should just get over it and move on. If that is the approach you elect to take then you probably are better off single and that will probably be your future status;

single.

The average woman wants to know why her husband was unfaithful and what can be done to ensure it doesn't happen again. Unfortunately or fortunately, depending on your perspective, this means that the process to getting back in her good graces is lengthy and difficult. Trust is a difficult thing to get back once it has been violated. The average woman wants to know the answer to all the who's, what's, where's, why's, when's and how's in order to grasps the concept of the infidelity and recover from it. Husbands must agree to provide all these answers and complete any actions necessary for the recovery process to be completed. If you are serious about repairing the marital relationship, you will hang in there for as long as it takes.

Ladies, if you were unfaithful to your husband, you will have some things to do as well to recover from the deception; however, the road to recovery is quite different. Since men do not think as we do, they also process the issues surrounding infidelity differently. The average husband does not want to know all the elements involved in the infidelity. They don't want to have any type of visualization of their wife with another man, unless they are into that type of thing; and that would be another subject for someone else to write about.

Ladies, you will have to prove your repentance by being willing and able to rebuild your husband's ego. There is a saying that states "a man wants a lady in the streets and a freak in the bed". Need I say more? Get your freak on and let your husband know that he is the only recipient of your wares. Communicate with him in the language that he best understands and that language is physical attraction and interaction. I'm not suggesting that men are that easy to recover from their wives being unfaithful, however, I am saying that if a man decides to forgive, the process to forgiveness is usually far less complicated. Ladies, if you were unfaithful, get use to the idea of your husband being concerned about where you are and who you are with. You cannot get offended if your husband starts to ask you questions that he didn't use to be concerned about before. He will pay attention to your attire like never before; so don't take it as a personal attack. Your husband may not want to know all the details about your previous infidelity but you better believe that he is paying attention and looking for any signs that you may be creeping again. Ladies, don't try to use your tears to manipulate your husband and don't try to get others involved in an effort to deflect responsibility for your actions. Most women learned at an early age that our tears are powerful and can often help us to avoid the penalties of our behavior. Ladies, we are not children anymore and we shouldn't resort to childish actions as adults. If you do not learn from your mistakes and accept the responsibility for them, you are setting yourself up for a repeat performance. You are also doing a disservice to your relationship if you try to shift the blame for your infidelity onto your spouse or others. As adults, we are responsible for our own actions and we should not try to avoid the consequences for situations that we engaged in of our own volition.

Trust will have to be earned back and both the husband and wife will have to commit to taking steps to get there together. It may seem like it is taking forever for the relationship to return to normal but before you know it you will realize that a significant amount of time has passed and it was not as difficult as you thought it would be. When we work hard for something, we tend to appreciate it more and take better care of it than we would have if it came easily. Absence can make the heart grow fonder but don't stay gone too long or the heart will wander.

Epilogue

Husbands and wives, once you have forgiven yourselves and each other for any marital issue to include unfaithfulness, stop bringing it up in conversation. There is no need to rehash old wounds once the wounds have healed. If you keep bringing up the hurts of the past that means you have not fully and truly forgiven. I'm not suggesting that you forget what happened; quite the contrary. Remember what happened but learn from what occurred and use those lessons to combat the potential of recurrence. Remember the pain that those situations caused and make a conscious effort not to repeat the behavior that led to the compromise. Deal with the past issues like you would a hot stove; don't touch it or you will get burned. Husbands and wives must realize that past events can serve a greater good and can be an experience that will teach others in a way that only first-hand knowledge can. I am a firm believer that all the things that my husband and I have experienced in the last 30 years has made us better as individuals and better as husband and wife.

Now that you have heard the real deal about marriage, I hope that you will use this information to avoid some of the unnecessary pitfalls that can lead to your marriage failure. Personally, I know our marriage survived by the grace of God, our commitment to making real changes, and our genuine love and respect for each other. Marriage is not something to be entered in to lightly and it is not something to be taken for granted. Marriage has to be built on a good foundation; otherwise the structure of marriage will not withstand the storms of life that will occur regardless of how many preventive measures are taken.

Everything that we have learned from this book should be shared with the one's we love. As I mentioned in the beginning, this book was inspired by my oldest daughter getting engaged. I challenge all husbands and wives to share all the details of this book and pass the knowledge along. Doing so can help to change the perception of marriage as a happily ever after type of fairytale. Couples need to know that marriage is work before they take their vows. The more time and effort spent preparing for marriage prior to walking down the aisle, the better equipped couples will be for having a successful and happy relationship.

Love is an action word that has to be revealed through words but also through deeds. Love is important but respect for yourself and your spouse is just as important if not more important. Happiness is real and is attainable if you are willing to do the work. Learn from the hiccups that will happen and recover from the disappointments that will occur. If you follow this advice, you will notice that the problems you experience will become fewer and further between.

Happiness is a conscious choice so choose to be happy. Choose to find the good things that can come out of every situation and choose to love with every part of your being without reservation. The real deal about marriage is that it's worth all the work and it has the potential to be mutually rewarding for both husband and wife.

Here is a little poem to help you on your journey to marital happiness:

Love is an important part of being
husband and wife.
But love alone is not enough to
recover from the pains of life.
You have to work hard and be
patient with the spouse you chose to live
with.
You have to be willing to jump
through hoops to regain the trust you
were careless with.
You have to know how important it
is to be faithful, honest, and truthful.
If you fail in any of these areas, you
must beg for forgiveness and be humble.
If you are willing and able to do
these things, I promise you the end will
be worth it.
A happy marriage to the man or
woman of your heart is something on
which you should never quit.

www.ingramcontent.com/pod-product-compliance
Lightning Source LLC
Chambersburg PA
CBHW062014040426
42447CB00010B/2020

9780990315605